How to Become an Old Codger.

Jeff Stevens

Jeff Stevens.

ISBN:1518665454
ISBN-13:9781518665455

DEDICATION

For Karen

Jeff Stevens.

Jeff Stevens.

Jeff Stevens.

Jeff Stevens.

ACKNOWLEDGMENTS

Thank you **Old Codgers** everywhere for all your unsuspecting input.

1 THE START OF OUR JOURNEY

So you have had the retirement party and waved a sad and fond farewell to all of your former colleagues and promised to" keep in touch?"

Good you have passed the first stage of Old Codgerism.

You may now think that having put your time in you can expect to put your feet up and take it easy?

No my friend, now commences perhaps the most challenging stage of your life; the switch from a perfectly fully functioning amiable human being into that peril of society the Old Codger.

You didn't think that *all* the old codgers that you see out and about are a natural phenomena did you?

Within these pages you will find the basic guide to making the transition from apprentice retiree to fully fledged old codger.

The phrase codger is thought to have derived from the word" cadger" which is quite appropriate as the art of cadging or borrowing without intent to return, is another skill you will learn as you progress.

The dictionary gives codger' as a man, especially an old or eccentric one: a term of affection or mild derision (often in the phrase old codger)'

Unfortunately in this modern emancipated society we now live in, the term is being corrupted to include that which was previously known as the 'old biddy.'

This all started with Emmeline Pankhurst and her ladettes demanding the right to lie in pools of their own alcohol provoked vomit.

This encroaching upon the previously male dominated men's club is to be regretted and fought at ever turn, though I confess it is a battle that we are destined to lose.

For the purpose of this guide we will try to keep to the male definition of the old codger, but I fear the rotund shadow of the old biddy will fall on us.

Before we commence a word of warning; we are aiming for the amiable slightly eccentric approach and not the psychotic barking mad 'old git' status.

To begin the transition we should perhaps give a thought to the old codger's apparel. You may have been a successful businessman in your previous existence who was well turned out in the latest designer menswear..... if you accept the challenge your learning curve will be steep.

Nor will the new age dolloper with seventeen kids from five different women seen on the High Street eating a meat and potato pasty and struggling to control a semi rabid Rottweiler/Ridgeback cross, fare any better.

No we are looking at the 'average working class man', who has 2 .4 children(no wonder the youngest is struggling) a wife and a semi mummified mother in law. He is nearer the finishing line than his well heeled counterpart and streets ahead of the Rab C Nesbitt wannabe.

You should be aiming for the utilitarian rather well used look; a shirt with a frayed collar is useful or at the very least one with a permanent soup stain on the front.

Your trousers should either be a size too small or a size too big, the choice is yours. They should also have an unidentified stain or two preferably on the upper thigh area.

If you opt for the larger size, a belt is a must; you are aiming for the 'old codger' look and not the 'phantom flasher' of local newspaper fame.

Incidentally you should also go for the zip fronted model, as this of course can be left at half mast, tempting but not revealing.

The buttoned version are a hazard only to be worn by the accomplished old codger as whilst it may be true 'a dead bird never leaves the nest', we should err on the side of caution. There is no gain in attracting the attention of that rarity; the local Police Officer.

Shoes are another article of free choice some codgers opt for the failed athlete look; a pair of scuffed trainers with at least one ripped side.

Myself I would suggest a well worn pair of leather Hush Puppies, black or brown are the colour choices, but if you decide on black shoes you must have brown laces and black laces for brown shoes. Please don't decide on the old piece of string trick, again we are going for the 'old codger' and not 'gentleman of the road' look.

Depending on the time of year your choices of top coat are as follows; in the warmer months you should consider a zip fronted windjammer type jacket(Google it). This can be multi pocketed, the more the merrier as we will see later.

During the colder months a longer coat is appropriate, this indeed could be worn over the summertime one to further hinder access. Please avoid at all times the just demobbed look; the khaki coat that your father used in the dog's basket, as this again can get you noticed by the transient Policeman, o.k. for you feminist Police *Officer*.

Head wear is again personal choice, traditionally the codger will go for the flat cap, either off white or with the loud chequered look.

Of late there is a modernist front that insists on wearing the imported baseball or sports cap.

Personally I think these are alien to our tradition, however if this is your choice go for the ones with the big logo e.g. NASA or NIKE. Avoid the jokey' I'm with stupid' type as the old codger is usually to be seen as a solitary figure.

I have seen people wearing either of these types with the addition of a pigeon or seagull feather, these look very fetching and are sure to gain the wearer public acclaim. Feathers are readily available outside any fast food takeaway.

The feathers are usually found in clumps and are all that remains after the cat/rat has had its repast.

Gloves are a good addition to the old codger's wear. They are obviously useful for keeping hands warm, but are also useful as a delaying tactic; this too will be discussed.

Finally in this codger's fashion advisory we come to the additional props. At the very least carry a large plastic shopping bag, again avoid dad's old gas mask haversack, these are now considered naff by fashionistas.

Ideally you could unearth one of those old wheeled shopping trolleys that were once the rage. Try to find one with a slightly oval wheel and loud squeak. This again is an important addition to your equipment and has several uses, all of which are befitting to an old codger's armoury.

Though initially you may consider a Zimmer frame as an accessory I would not advise this, as you are stepping across the thin divide between old codger and permanent Nursing Home resident, avoid this as long as possible, though eventually it *may* come to this but remember you still have...er, well months of active life ahead.

You may also consider a simple walking stick, handy for holding out at bus stops or tripping would be queue jumpers.

A small dog will also be of use but avoid the be ribboned Yorkshire Terrier as a crowd of old biddies and male hairdressers will gather.

One of those long retractable leads will also help, they are very entertaining when allowed to tangle around numerous legs.

We have discussed your attire and accessories, there is now a word on your personal appearance.

Ideally you will be either bald or partially defoliated by now.

Yes we've all seen the 'what a good head of hair he has' brigade, these anomalies should be treated with caution; is it their own hair and not belonging to some impoverished Mexican peon?

They are a lost cause and will cling to their long ago youth like an octopus on heat.

They can be heard to tell enquirers that they are in their' late 40's.' Avoid these traitors to the cause.

Your nose and ear hair should be of a comparative length and should be visible from around 5 yards or so.

Ideally the nose hair should have a dewdrop on each protrusion, or to go for the really old fashioned look a yellow brown coating of snuff, though this is seldom seen in these health conscious days, however a good non toxic substitute is custard powder, liberally coated as our pin-up Mary Berry would say.

The perfect look is if you are lucky enough to have an odd hair or two sprouting half way down the outside of your nose(or half way up if you are an optimist).

Unfortunately this is in the lap of the gods, but fingers crossed you could be blessed.

Eyebrows are a good codger identifier. Go for the Sir Patrick Moore or Denis Healey type; the wild and wooly.

Incidentally Denis is often referred to as 'the best Prime Minister we never had.'

Well can I go on record as the best England striker we never had?

Or (go for it) 'the first British man on the moon we never had.'

The list is limitless really .

2 QUEUING

The art of queuing is considered to be one of the most useful skills that the old codger can master. Though of late the United Kingdom has seen the art come under a relentless attack from foreign influences, the old codger will still have a use for it.

The rot set in with cheap foreign holidays becoming the norm, prior to this we of the island nation were happy to queue for hours just to be told that the last loaf had gone(luckily you can still experience this on some holidays in the former USSR).

We learned to queue at school whether it was for the nauseating 'but nourishing' school dinners, or indeed for a healthy dose of corporal punishment. 'Bend over boy!'

I could never understand this latter orderly queuing, where we exchanged snippets of whispered information, 'how many are you down for?'

'Oh just the ten', would be the cheery reply.

A good trick was available if you were to be followed by a younger initiate after your own punishment.

On receiving your corporal dose you would leave the Head's study and pretend to be refastening your trousers, the younger boy in a panicky state would start to unfasten his own and hopefully drop them on entering the study, to be greeted by an equally panicked Headmaster.

Nowadays that wouldn't happen as it's all done via the internet.

The more travelled younger generation have all but abandoned queuing, mini riots at sales are now the norm, but there is still a place for you in the codger queue.

The basic rules of old codger queuing are simple; you must never rush but develop a shambling zigzag approach. Nowadays with many post offices and airports adapting their own versions of this, it isn't any longer an individual sport, but there is still fun to be had.

A good place to start is the bus stop queue; the best kind are the larger enclosed shelters. People cannot easily avoid you under the confined spaces. You can exhaust your theory of global warming being caused by cows farting(look it up)to any interested or indeed uninterested party.

Be aware of your audience, those consisting of mainly teenagers or Social Workers will consider you an 'old git' rather than the embraceable old codger that you aspire to.

Also avoid Nuns, Parish Priests or Scientologists, they will be less likely to listen and more likely to try to cast out your devils.

Once you get to the front of the queue ready to board the bus you have an option; stand there looking bemused and ask,' is this the bus to.....? You must have first ensured that it isn't of course, then ask the driver to list which stops the bus does indeed stop at.

You may ask for a repeat if you are feeling particularly chipper, but once is usually suffice.

This can be the main course or you can combine it with the more bemused look as you begin to rifle through your multiple pocketed coat for your wallet(ideally after struggling to remove your gloves).

This is usually found sans bus pass, so again you rummage through even more pockets, before producing it with a flourish only to be told that it is:

a) Out of date. b) Not yours. c) Your Tesco club card.

You should then immediately decide to 'fancy a walk anyway'.

A female variant of this behavior is of course the possessor of a cavernous handbag the volume of which is second only to a mid sized camper van, however it is a brave codger who would carry a man bag, unless of course he is Jack Bauer or has had a colostomy.

Supermarkets are another happy hunting ground as people are usually in a rush. One trick is to place yourself on the corner of an aisle with the trolley blocking the path. A barricade will soon form as traffic passes around you. If you are lucky you can strike up a conversation with a like minded soul and hold forth on how busy the store is.

On reaching the checkout the already mentioned fumbled pocket search can again take place during which you recall that you haven't picked up those special offer toilet rolls. You can then leave the checkout blocked because the till operator(no sexism here) has put your purchases into the system, this is a good way to block the tills, but don't overdo it as once again you are bordering on 'old git' status.

On your return stride confidently past the twenty people in the queue smile and pay for your goods.

I prefer a wallet for my cash as my Grandfather used to say, 'never trust a Welshman or a man with a purse!'

Mind you he did also say,' Horse muck's tuppence a bag.'

If you wish you can ask the harassed operator ,'are bags for life just for pensioners?'

Quickly leave the store and then repeat the pocket shuffle at the taxi/bus queue. Returning home you can be well satisfied on another successful old codger's outing.

HOBBIES

Now whilst we may quite rightly say that being an old codger is a hobby in itself, we should also realise that there are many variants to this theme some of which follow.

PHOTOGRAPHY.

In this digital age that we find ourselves meandering in, it has never been easier or more affordable to participate in this popular hobby. There are a couple of ways to do this.

The first is jump in with both feet into the new all singing all dancing digital camera malarkey.

The advantage to this is almost everyone takes photographs, be it with a dedicated camera or on their latest smart phone, so you have a vast number of people you can ask for advice.

The basic starter method is to buy a cheap mobile phone from e-bay or another online market. You must ensure that the 'phone is one with a camera included, this of course should be broken thus rendering any helper's instruction worthless.

A second option is to buy an older 'phone without a camera these can readily be purchased in parts of Yorkshire or across the big border in Scotland, where the people are 'careful' with their pennies. The idea is to ask anyone that you should encounter,

'Can you just give me an idea how to take photos with my new 'phone?"

This can readily pass a few hours each and every day.

You can of course opt for an expensive *real* digital camera and allow the helper to blind you with science, before you ask him to repeat his comments.

Let him begin his banter, nod and smile reassuringly at regular intervals, then casually ask him where you can buy film for the camera.

A variant of this is to produce Grandfather's Box Brownie and go into any large store's digital camera section and ask for film.

I am sure that once you learn the ropes you will discover your own favourite methods for allowing people to 'help' you.

MOTORING.

Motoring? You ask, in this day and age, a hobby?
Well yes the roads are nowadays more or less giant car parks but
there is still sport to be had.

With all the namby pamby 'Save the World Brigade's' restrictions on
vehicle emissions, we can no longer leave an annoying Royal Navy
like smokescreen behind us. That's unless you are an eastern
European wagon driver of course.
You should perhaps avoid the 'old codger in motion' tricks until you
become more comfortable with the various abuse.
'White Van Man ' should be left alone as he is more than likely to
have tattoos that are more muscular than your entire old codger
body.
At best keep him waiting at traffic lights, with practice you can delay
your progress to leave him stranded at the lights as they change.
Remember to wave a casual apology as you accelerate into second
gear.
 Don't overdo this, as after three times you are toying with becoming
an ornament on the van's bonnet.
Also make sure that the white van in your rear view mirror doesn't
also have all those funny day glow chequers on as you may delay the
district's only rapid response vehicle from delivering the chips.

You can also cause chaos at the filling station make a careful note of which side of the car the petrol cap is on, then drive to the pumps that are on the opposite side.

With luck the petrol filler pipe won't reach, although of late some filling stations have made their pumps codger proof by extending the pipe's reach.

Don't worry though you can always be seen trying to fathom out the intricacies of paying the bill with the pump's card option. This is good for a few minutes, then you should make an exaggerated gesture with your hands as though asking for divine intervention before doing the walk of shame to the garage's shop.

Once there you again have an option; pay straight away smiling apologetically, or you can vent your theories on the usurping of the British worker by the evil machines.

'The world is your lobster ', as Arthur Daley once said.

BIRD WATCHING.

Bird watching is ideal for the nosey old codgers amongst us. You can purchase an old pair of binoculars; go for the ex-Royal Naval W.W.2 type that are about two feet long(alright 60 cm.)

These along with the British Bird Watching Pocket Guide will keep you occupied for ,oh say half an hour or so.

The rest of the time you can people watch, though this is discouraged within two miles of the local High School or ladies outdoor aerobic session!

Incidentally(you knew there was going to be one.) I think that we codgers should band together and completely reject that foreign invader the Metric System.

You and I suffered many a beating at school learning our weights and measures in good old Anglo Saxon-Jute-Viking-Roman Imperial measure. What was wrong with:

Length:
Inch [2.54 cm]
Link = 7.92 inches
Foot = 12 inches [30.48 cm]
Yard = 3 feet [91.44 cm]
Rod, Pole or Perch = 25 links = 5½ yards [about 5 metres]
Chain = 22 yards = 66 feet = 100 Links [length of a cricket wicket, about 20 metres]
Furlong = 10 chains = 220 yards [length of a furrow, about 200 metres]
Mile = 8 furlongs = 1760 yards = 5280 feet [a thousand Roman paces

Nothing! I blame the Channel Tunnel. I genuinely struggle with these Johnny Foreigner measurements, no acting of befuddlement is necessary.

If like myself, you worked in the publishing industry it was a double - whammy. I had also to learn interesting measurements such as Quad Demy. Octavo. Crown etc. Coupled with learning the different point sizes of typefaces for nigh on six years, I was less than ecstatic when decimalisation crept in c. February 15th.1971.

Such is progress!

TRAIN SPOTTING.

No, no; even the old codger should have his pride!

'Oh look, it's a double gauge, quadruple mounted shiny painted thingy bob triple pinned, double shackled number 60121.'
NO, IT'S A TRAIN!

Though to be politically correct it is a Steam Locomotive pulling other wheeled carriages that form a train......Sheesh!

The Americans may have Air Force One to convey their Head Honcho, but we have this.
Cower in terror you enemies of the United Kingdom!

ICT(Information and Communications Technology)

Whilst some of our silver haired brigade may consider computers to be a somewhat scary prospect to indulge as a hobby, you should take the plunge.

This will open up a whole new world for you.

There are two ways to go about this; the first is the independent effort; buy a computer and jump in.

The second and possibly more entertaining way is to join a I.C.T. class.

Many community centres and colleges run free courses for the senior citizens, please note it is no longer P.C. to refer to old codgers as old age pensioners.

Breaking News! The latest guideline now states we are now 'older adults.'

The centres also provide a tutor to teach in a very informal way. You will learn the basics; how to switch the computer on and log on to the computer, conduct web searches and access lots of useful information.

The tutors vary in their abilities from the expert to the inept; one tutor of my acquaintance had to be shown how to switch the wall mounted power sockets on!

When you start to learn the ins and out of computing do not be deterred by the continual criticism of your spellings or grammar by the clever clogs Microsoft spell checker.

It will tell you many times that you have spelled a word wrong. Do not despair this is America claiming world domination by subversive means.

You may of course have used computers for years either in your former occupation or as home user.

The ICT class can still be attended you can use it to hone your skills or more likely embarrass the tutor with your questions.

As the tutor explains the cursor to the class of newbies ask innocently ,"How do I change the cursor's appearance?"

Or you could surreptitiously change the keyboard's configuration to another country's; select the Canadian French for starters.

Having lit the blue touch paper stand back as the tutor flounders as he or she tries to 'help the learner.'

You may soon tire of their ineptitude, so now you could use your time and skills to help the genuine learners and the tutor to achieve success, you may feel a better person in doing so.

The internet opens up a whole new world for the old codger, there are many local sites were the members debate such important topics as the lack of pooper scooper bins in your area.

You may join in the debate or lurk voyeuristically in the background without comment, the choice is yours.

These sites can in fact be a conduit for public opinion. It is not unknown for the less active journalist to peruse such sites for snippets of news to pursue as their latest scoop.

You could of course start a topic off and see how it runs....

"Was that Lord Lucan?"

This could open a can of worms, as this could lead to a new career on the 'Sunday Sport.'

A word of caution to the new codger internet user; those of us who like to imbibe in a little snifter in the evening would be wise not to mix this with internet use.

It is a known fact that alcohol + internet + credit card= Trouble!

A couple of days after this combo you could answer the doorbell and find a baker's dozen of ceramic garden gnomes on your doorstep this is unnerving especially to the non garden house owners amongst us. Even worse, try explaining to your wife the arrival of ' Monica from Latvia', with her suitcase and twins in tow one fine morning.

GARDENING

When you have acquired your collection of gnomes, they are good for keeping you company whilst you indulge in another old codger favourite pastime; gardening!

Like most hobbies and pastimes you can approach this in two ways. You can have a wonderful well groomed garden in which you can spend hour after hour polishing your grass and awaiting next door's cat's toilet excursion.

Or you can do the bare minimum having paved over the grass and covered your flower beds in gravel.

I recommend the latter as this will free you to spend time on the true pursuit of gardeners, i.e. communication.

You can harangue your neighbour about his afore mentioned feline's unsanitary habit. This is good for a half hour or so but you should always preface your rehearsed speech with, 'I don't like to complain, but....'

This will defuse any potential serious fallouts, remember 'old codger' status and not 'old git' is what we are striving for.

The neighbour will be apologetic and you will have points stored for any future mishaps e.g. the day your grandchild decides to pick next door's prize roses 'for mummy' .

The main entertainment can be derived from conversations with passersby, many will be familiar from daily contact.

There will be the new breed of 'yummy mummies' who pass as they take their little ones to school.

Mostly these will consist of tiny females driving what appear to be military Humvees, so no conversations there , although you are on hand to act as witness to the inevitable fender bender.(See America is at it again.)

There will of course be the occasional walking parent. They are usually too harassed to speak having finally found little Damien's gym kit lying unwashed in that new wicker basket they bought from Argos Sometimes the kid's feet seem to levitate as they are dragged past in the rush to queue at the school entry.

Hopefully you will also get the passing newbie, these vary from the innocent dog walker to that most welcome of all callers, the Jehovah's Witnesses.

Over the years I have accumulated piles of Watch Tower like leaflets and pamphlets. These are excellent bedding material for your grand children's rabbit or hamster.

Don't forget to shred these first.

'Oh! You meant the paper, Grandad.'

Meanwhile back to the garden; another useful way of time wasting is to be asked directions by any confused passersby.

These can be placed into two categories; the straight forward polite request for help, which you respond to with best of your ability, sending the grateful traveler on his or her way.

The second more entertaining is the arrogant demand for assistance. This character tries to make you regret living in such a confusing area.

They are a temptation to the soul and must be punished.

For example if you meet such a stroppy demand for help, always send them either onto the nearest motorway, or into the local big town's one way system.

Your aim is not to help but to ensure that they become even more lost and find it impossible to return to harangue you for misdirection. You may find that if they do find their way back to you then they may become abusive.

The way to handle this is to remain calm, hopefully they will pick on that old chestnut 'the village idiot', handle as follows.

The car/person arrives back at your garden, and immediately accuses you of being the village idiot, you pause think for a moment or two. You then respond.

A) 'Oh no that be my brother, he's the clever one!'

B) 'Oh no it's only a small village and we all take turns, it be the vicar today!'

They will usually cut their losses and leave, but be prepared to flee quickly.

The Village Idiot?

I have a confession on this subject; in reality I live in an area where all the streets are named after flowers; Hyacinth, Bluebell, Narcissus and the like.

This make any attempt at giving directions a nightmare.

So my solution if accosted by any lost soul, is to shrug apologetically and tell them that I am only working there for the day.

I have got away with this for over 30 years man and boy or codger and codgling as they are now known.

Mind you my wife gets some funny looks from the lesser known neighbours.

Curtains twitch, 'that workman's there again!'

I have had a non-sense of direction all my life, my wife says that I am the only person she knows who gets lost in our local supermarket.
Perhaps I have been in codger training all my adult life?

Sometimes it pays to admit at an earlier stage that you are lost!

You can also spend your time in the garden becoming the hub of a thriving cadger empire. You are only living up to your historical title of old cadger, now modernised to codger.

This is initiated by asking to borrow for example your neighbour's long reach electric hedge trimmers.

You then use this most useful tool before lending it to another neighbour in exchange for use of his new leaf sucker/blower. This in turn can be exchanged for a spin on yet another neighbour's new ride on mower.

If you pace yourself and use sound judgement you may one day find yourself with a weeks time share apartment in Tenerife.

Just remember where everything actually lives!

SINGING ANYONE?

Those of us who are musically minded may consider joining the local codger choir.

This usually consists of around a dozen old biddies with a smattering of males to give choral depth.

You will meet once or twice a week the group will usually be led by an old biddy with aspirations to be the next Gracie Fields.

Sadly in truth she sounds more like a tomcat on a vet visit to have its reproductive assets removed.

The songs you will learn will all be out of your vocal range, though you could try miming.

This will work for a while until the leader decides to have you all singing solos.

However don't despair there are numerous choirs around the country that despite many years of practice still inflict their tuneless pain on their captive audiences.

They appear at church functions, pensioner's parties and the occasional funeral.

Our local choir used to appear at Tesco, until the Store Manager noted the correlated fall in sales on those particular appearance days. Who knows they may have been hired by Asda?

It's a cutthroat sales world out there!

In passing I would like to place on record my thanks to Pierce Brosnan, this former James Bond has made it socially acceptable to appear in public and 'sing' like a laryngitis stricken frog.

His rendition of Abba's 'SOS' in the movie Mama Mia was a landmark performance and gave encouragement to millions of tone deaf flat voiced singers.

But please no encores!

MUSICAL INSTRUMENTS.

With more times on your hands you may seize the chance to learn a new skill; how about mastering a musical instrument.

The types of instrument though legion are in fact somewhat limited by your now advanced age.

The Tuba though a splendid instrument is best left to those of us who have healthy lungs ,low blood pressure and a strong sphincter muscle.

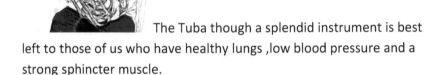

The would be rock god should remember that it takes years to perfect the guitar. In the meantime your fingers will bleed and swell, though this can be useful for avoiding the dishwashing duties.

The piano is also a difficult instrument to master. Would be codger players could find that they may run out of time.

I have, after many years searching found that I have now mastered an instrument. You should give it a try!

But watch out for the old repetitive strain injury.

SHOPPING

Now many of you will have considered this topic a female pastime. The female can disappear for a full days shopping only to return some hours later with nothing but sore feet as a reward.

This is in preference to your wife maxing out your credit card, the only expenditure having been numerous stops for fuelling i.e. tea or coffee and cakes.

But there are areas where the old codger comes into his own.

WH Smith's stores are an ideal place for this with the narrow spaced aisles the store is ideal for a spot of browsing.

There is a large collection of magazines, DVD's and books to browse, you and like minded souls can spend hours becoming experts in the fields of Radio Control Modelling or Scuba Diving(all in a non participating way of course.)

Add a Jack Bauer bag around your shoulders and you can block the aisles with confidence.

Your only problem will be that nemesis of the codger browser; the mother and baby buggy.

The innocent browser will suffer scuffed ankles and potential damage to his crown jewels, as she bludgeons her way past.

Many is the time I have contemplated super gluing the buggy brakes in the locked position, but one look at the Boadicea bodied mother instantly dissuades me.

ROLL MODELS.

When we consider those luminaries who have influenced the old codger, we perhaps turn our minds to that hero of the underdog, Victor Meldrew.

This wonderful character played with panache by the great Richard Wilson, was an icon for the old codger a few years ago.

Yet even Victor had feet of clay; he may have been past the flush of youth(preparing for the many flushes of old age),but he was in fact not a pensioner but a redundant security guard in his mid fifties. Nevertheless he is to many the epitome of the flat capped old codger; disgruntled, annoying, bad tempered but with an inner sense of decency. Long may he be repeated on the television.

Perhaps another icon was Uncle Albert of the series 'Only fools and Horses' fame.

His constant ramblings of, 'during the war.....' was a master class in codger behaviour. Sadly the actor who played him; Buster Merryfield has left us, dying in 1999.

Another roll model that springs to mind is that 'Greatest Englishman.'

Sir Winston Spencer Churchill.

This mega star had it all; he drank like a fish, was surly natured but at the same time evoked devotion. He had the ideal appearance, with jutting jaw, florid complexion and middle aged paunch he looked like an old bar bruiser. Yet his speeches and writings are still held up as the work of genius over 50 years later.

I think Victor, Albert and Winnie would have got on very well.

CHRISTMAS

Sooner or later the old codger will have to face up to the seasonal request of ,'would you be our Santa?'

Nowadays this request is as likely to come from a nursing home as a nursery.

Taking these in reverse order, if you are requested by a nursery group then chances are you will be thoroughly vetted by the local authorities as to your suitability and have had your background searched for criminal records.

No, owning up to a collection of Des O'Connor albums doesn't count.

Once you have been vetted, you will be given the uniform. This will consist of a paper like material that rips as you try to put it on.

Hopefully your ahem, mature figure will fill out the suit to Santa like proportions.

You should also root out your old gardening wellingtons, remembering to clean off next door's cats contribution.

The first test is the beard, this will be like wearing a rancid dead ferret on your face.

The elastic that holds this in position will force the ferret up into your nasal passages until you are continually sneezing and snuffling.

Your voice ideally should have the correct vocal depth associated with Santa's, 'Ho! Ho! Ho!'

Though in reality the asthma attack that the ferret beard has brought on will limit this to a nasal, 'Oh! Oh! Oh!'

Your hopes of maintaining your street cred as Santa with fall at the first hurdle.

I was once volunteered to be Santa for a local women and children's group. I prepared the best that I could and everything seemed fine until I donned the ferret beard.

I think the last wearer(or two) had been eating a curry whilst wearing the disguise as the thing absolutely reeked.

Anyhow in I went to greet the kids who were all around six or seven years of age, I passed the gifts out reading each name out correctly with the help of a Santa's helper.

I had noticed one little boy sat near to me gazing with what I assumed was fascination in meeting Santa.

Our eyes met and he gazed at me with an angelic look on his face and bawled out, 'I can see the elastic on your beard!'

My face went as red as my suit, luckily the rest of the kids were more interested in their gifts than the weirdo imposter.

 Off I went coughing and sneezing. 'Oh! Oh! Oh!

So perform for youngsters at your peril, best I think to go dressed as an elf who is helping Santa distribute gifts.

Now older Santa customers i.e. nursing home residents are a different kettle of fish.

The men can't be drawn into the Christmas spirit that you are representing and the women, well suffice to say keep your crown jewels out of reach!

Whilst not exactly in their second childhood some of them are in their second early twenties!

They don't need mistletoe to pounce on you, just a clear run.

 But as the late great Frankie Howerd used to say, "we mustn't mock."

For all we know the nursing home may be our future so best to grin and bear it and pick up a few tips whilst you are there.

SOCIALISING.

Now this pastime can be the most enjoyable of all, though there are a few points to consider.

Do we plan to socialise with our better half? Or does she have an old biddy group to attend?

Are you planning on joining any organised groups? I believe Tai Chi can be very rewarding but it is not to be recommended to those with any degree of flatulence.

All that poised serene standing on one leg can be ruined forever with just one gaseous release. Mind you I have knowledge of some old biddies who could run you a close second.

Very great care must be taken and lay off the spicy foods and in particular the cabbage soup diet .This could result in a visit from the Chemical Warfare boys.

Beware the Cabbage Soup Diet!

Many local Community Centres will provide a happy hunting ground for the sociable codger.

Some provide exercise classes for the 'young at heart'(and stiff of limb.) I have even spotted 'Walking pace Five aside Football.' Now there's a challenge if I ever saw one.

Thankfully you could go on ad infinitum about the offside rule; safe in the knowledge that no-one else would have a clue about the veracity of your arguments. A bit like the House Of Lords really!

For those seeking a gentler pastime we have dominoes, darts and pool often provided with a session or two of Bingo to keep the ladies happy.

Years ago I used to play dominoes against a blind chap, I never ever won a game. I don't know how or why, though I had my suspicions about the small dog that accompanied him.

The game of darts is another splendid way to pass your time. Though caution is required if you intend to use the time in winding up your fellow players.

This is not recommended unless you want to become a human pin cushion.

Remember your fellow players may well be 7th Dan exponents of the old codger black arts.

The 'causal chuck' can prove to be very annoying if carried out with accuracy.

Every now and again the community centre/social club will have what our own grannies called 'a get together.' This consists of the resourceful biddies making sandwiches and sausage rolls with perhaps a fairy cake to follow.

During this entertainment you will have a sing-a-long. Now you and I may have grown up rocking to Queen, Slade, Black Sabbath or the like, but mark my words your sing-a -long will consist of old World War Two songs. Vera Lynn, George Formby and those upstarts Flanagan and Allen will feature strongly.

It is as though once we pass the retirement age our DNA melds into some great universal false memory.

We weren't around during the war why do we sing 'all the old favourites?'

Will the next generation be smitten by the likes of 1950's Clarence 'Frogman Henry or Johnny Ray?

I think not, but we of the present ranks are stuck in the time warp of WW2.

Don't fight it join in and sing your heart out it's good for the soul!

Usually the social club will have an Alpha male and an equally formidable female second in command.

No matter what the thoughts of the collective group, these two will dominate the entertainment. Hence the WW2 re-enactment.

I once attended a function or 'do' as that's how they refer to all social gatherings. (Except possibly funerals; they are too near to the final doorway to get too enthusiastic.

Anyhow ,the function was in full swing when one of the older male attendees had an epileptic fit. A space quickly appeared around the smitten soul, as the first aider administered what comfort he could. Eventually an ambulance arrived and the crew were soon treating the poor man.

As I looked on at the scene, I became aware of a presence by my side.

Well actually I became aware due to a walking stick being sharply tapped against my ankle bone. I turned to see Keith the ancient Alpha male sadly shaking his head, I took this to be a display of sympathy or indeed empathy.

This was quickly dispelled when he shook his head once more and said, 'this'll never do we have a turn coming on in a minute!'

As the patient was being loaded onto the ambulance's trolley, music struck up (it was 'On the Good Ship Lollipop' as sung by Shirley Temple.)

A vision of loveliness, namely Rosemary; Keith's equally ancient partner in crime appeared dressed in gold hot pants and waist length blonde wig, she started dancing and miming to the song.

Immediately the audience lost interest in the ambulance malarkey and applauded Rosemary and her lollipop.

The ambulance crew quietly left with the patient as the turn continued.

It just goes to show that some are natural born codgers of M.A. standards, or cap and gown as they used to say around here.

Another potential codger gathering is the 'Coach Trip.' This can be of great entertainment, you will be with like minded peers(more of that soon)and may travel on the 'chara'(derived from the French Charabanc; meaning conveyance for coffin dodgers.)

Now the standard seating of a bog-standard coach is 56 seats(no pun is rejected.)

This means that the potential for arguments is an equation only Einstein could work out. Was he an old codger? Well he had the outward appearance of one but his mind was far too focused to qualify for our purposes.

Sid and Barbara want to sit across from the driver but so do the Alphas; so no contest there, after all the driver will need directing. The directions will consist of which motorway service stations can serve as emergency pit-stops in the event of one of our peers, well wanting to pee!

With 56 ancients on board with various bowel and bladder problems, the driver better be on his game.

There are new fangled coaches with toilet facilities on board, but again the Alpha male has parsimoniously rejected the idea of an extra £20 that this would cost.

This is approximately a third of the extra cost of fuel that the coach company will expend searching out watering holes.

An earlier excursion.

Tactics are discussed at length.

HOLIDAYS

Holidaying for the codger opens up a whole new world of adventures and challenges.

The first challenge is what to take with us; should we travel light or take everything but the kitchen sink?

Considering airport security as it is of late, I would opt for the light and easily scanned items.

It is not advisable to have coils of charger wires appearing on the x ray scanner.

You could of course over pack your main luggage and then spend a merry twenty minutes repacking at the check in area. This is perfectly acceptable codger behaviour but you could end up wearing as many clothing layers as an Eskimo.

If your choice of luggage items are questioned then you should immediately don your confused elderly gentleman's persona with no signs of stroppy behaviour.

Otherwise you could be shown to a small room wherein awaits a gorilla sized security employee with marigolds covering his shovel sized hands!

Having finally negotiated the airport's strange customs(see again no pun is refused)you will finally have time to wander around the shops within the airside area.

What used to be a bargain hunters happy hunting ground has of late lost a lot of its appeal due to the growth of the Common Market, EEC or European Union whatever the title of the week is nowadays, we seem to have lost the "duty free "offers.

Indeed I have found the cost of various items having a rather large mark up on the prices that you would encounter on the High Street. Such is progress!

I have noticed that if some of the queuing passengers have 'mobility problems' they are allowed on the plane before the more able bodied. The codger is well placed to enhance his lack of fitness, shuffling up to the check-in desk.

The staff will probably ignore the fact that you should have notified the airline of your problems prior to your airport arrival and class you as a priority passenger.

The only downside to this queue jumping, is that as a less mobile passenger, you will after the flight have to remain on the plane until the more able have left.

Now you can try the mid flight miracle approach; leaping to your feet and shouting ,"Hallelujah ,it's a miracle," then run up and down the aisle. This should be risk assessed as in this current paranoid travellers age we live in, chances are that you will be pounced on by several members of a travelling Fijian Rugby team and then restrained for the rest of the flight.

Once on the plane you will join the interminable wait for your fellow passengers to load their carry on luggage into the overhead storage areas.
It always amazes me that some people have carry on bags that are the same size as my hold luggage!
When this ritual has been performed you will be seated only to find that your travelling companion is what our American cousins refer to as a "lard ass."
This translates into "so that's who ate all the pies."
Man or woman, their obese folds of fat will overwhelm you as you travel, your circulation will begin to fail as they spread out encroaching into your personal space.
Things will only get worse as the cabin crew begin to sell their wares. Is it only me that gets to be the meat in the sandwich between lard ass and rotund cabin crew?
God help you if your inner plumbing is crying for the relief of the cupboard sized toilet.
Grit your teeth(and buttocks) and pray that the delay is brief.

Whilst we are still in the air, again is it only me that find the cabin crew's safety demonstrations somewhat condescending?
Recently some airlines in an effort to attract our undivided attention, have decided to show recordings of child actors demonstrating the various procedures, how very apt.
If we are crashing from 38,000 feet no amount of brace positioning is going to help you, indeed with the configuration of seating you cannot adopt the position.
As for the life jacket drill, again descending from aloft in a rather rapid way...how many of us could actually don a life jacket?
It is all a con to reassure the nervous flier.........hang on that's me!
 Oh well happy journey!

Codgers on holiday can usually be separated into two groups; the ones who act their age or more likely the "there's life in the old dog yet type".

They will party until midnight ,then limp off to bed leaving the floor to the next generation ,but be up at the crack of dawn to claim their sun lounger spot before the Germans arise.

An uneasy peace exist between our codgers and the Germans; for though we didn't personally participate in the last fisticuffs ,we were brought up on tales of battles with the "Huns".

Thanks mainly to comics like Victor, Eagle and Hotspur we grew up with a stereotype image of the German nation, namely an arrogant master race.

I have to say that the ones I have met whilst holidaying are friendly and polite and rarely click their heels together whilst introducing themselves.

Perhaps we will be the last generation of our respective nations to be wary of each other?

After all we now have the Isis crisis to worry about on our holidays. Pretty soon the only 'safe choice' will be the Shetlands or Outer Hebrides, let's see the buggers trying to find their way to there!

If you are of a gregarious nature, then chances are you will attract the hotel bores.

I find that on your first morning's meal in the hotel you should limit your conversation with any fellow diners to a disgruntled," morning." Anything other than this and you will be marked for boredom as sure as if you are painted by a ballistic laser.

The H.B(hotel bores) with descend on you at every opportunity, you will learn about Harold's haemorroids and Mabel's latest gynaecological operation, usually this will be as you are consuming your bacon and runny egg.

If you don't repel these boarders on the first incursion you are lost. You will find yourselves exchanging addresses, after spending the whole holiday trying to avoid them only to fail at every turn.

How to do this you ask?

Well there are a couple of ways.

You could on the second encounter pucker up and give Harold a welcoming kiss, this will normally deter him from pursuing your acquaintance. Though again this should be risk assessed as there are some strange couples out there.

More reliable is the old pepper trick, inhale this on their approach and sneeze whole heartedly in their direction. Then whilst wiping them down with a small folded tissue mutter an apology saying this only came on after your trip to the Congo and how you hope it's not the Dengue fever again.

This usually works, but again it has its perils as you could be sharing the flight home with the couple who just might feel it their duty to report the risk to the airline authorities.

Who knows you could have an extended holiday albeit in the isolation ward.

VOLUNTARY WORK

On returning from your holiday, batteries fully charged you will now be ready to renter the fray of old codgerism.

You may find that you have too much time on your hands and consider voluntary work.

There are many variations on this theme; from simply helping a less mobile neighbour to fully fledged Royal Voluntary Service superstar volunteer.

You could volunteer at the local hospital(well local as in 20 miles away) to work in their visitors cafe or be a trolley dolly with cups of tea for the patients.

These tasks are best carried out by codgers with what my old Gran used to refer to as 'a sunny outlook' and not by those of us with less charisma than Piers Morgan.

You shouldn't really apply if you resemble the above, although if the hospital has a Psychiatric Department you may be able to find the help that you need.

Another idea would be to volunteer for the School Crossing Patrol, this worthy pastime will fall into two categories ; the first considered a lost cause by many, will consist of road duty outside a High School. You will spend half your time looking for your patrol lollipop, that you had left hidden in a nearby garden ,only to find that one of your school goers has removed it and stuck it on top of the bus shelter or if you are really unlucky a passing continent bound lorry .
The rest of the time will be spent being verbally abused by that flower of British manhood ; the lesser spotted teenager.
The second group is the youngsters who have just started school, they will most likely treat you with far more respect giving you a cheery greeting each day and even calling you by your actual name and not some demeaning nickname as the older group might.
I wonder what happens to *some* of the youngsters in the ten years or so at school?
Generally speaking they mutate from pleasant children into foul mouthed, ill mannered yobs with the I.Q. of a pencil. Do they have this as an extra subject nowadays?

Health.

We've touched on the subject of health; mainly the increased ratio of toilet visits.

You may be one of the lucky ones with an iron like constitution, but more likely you will have at least a few twinges to contend with.

It is often said that in later life our body pays for our earlier life; it's an extension of 'we are what we eat.'

Well as far as I am concerned I must have consumed all of the pies on offer!

In a later life desire to keep fit we will be advised to lose that spare tyre and exercise more this is probably good advice but somewhat belated. If I was able to lose weight and exercise more, then surely I wouldn't be in this dilapidated state to start with!

You could try buying one of those latest must have gadgets, a personal fitness wristband. There are many variations on this theme, but they basically all do the same thing; tracking your activity levels heartbeat and sleeping patterns.

It can be used to track how many paces you walk and calories burned as you make your way to the local pub. No doubt there is a gadget that tells you how many calories your three pints consumed contain. On balance you would probably lose more weight abstaining and staying at home.

My own device records my sleep patterns, it states how many hours sleep and waking periods I have during the night. Disconcertingly I seem to burn more calories toilet trotting than I do walking in the daytime!

In combination with a smart phone and social media it is possible to publish online your walking distance and route each day. Surely this is a stalkers paradise.

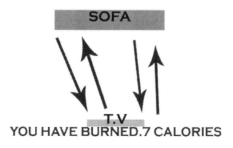

YOU HAVE BURNED.7 CALORIES

Ditch that T.V.remote and watch the pounds melt away.

It's like everything else what is good for you today will be deemed bad for you by next year.

I am old enough to remember the advertising slogans, 'go to work on an egg and drinka pint a milk a day.'

These were both later considered harmful to good health, though eggs are now back as a wonder food.

Do we listen to advice at our peril?

After all it's not that long ago that tobacco companies were encouraging us to smoke their cancer sticks:

Strand Cigarettes. Advertising slogan; ' You're never alone with a Strand!'

Chesterfield Cigarettes.' Blow some my way!'

Senior Service.' A product of the Master Mind. Senior Service Satisfy.'

Finally the wonderful Camel Cigarettes .' More Doctors smoke Camels than any other cigarette! I'd walk a mile for a Camel!'

We would probably have been better off smoking Camel dung.

I have never actually smoked, but as a younger man I probably passively inhaled as much smoke as a twenty a day man.

Is it too late for legal action?

HAVE YOU SEEN THIS MAN?

A VISIT TO THE DOCTORS.

On a recent visit to my doctors surgery I was booked in to see a newer member of staff that I hadn't previously met.

I told him of my ailment and what I was worried was wrong.

His jocular response was, 'oh have we been consulting Doctor Google?'

Well yes doctor I had, as he didn't make me wait two weeks for an appointment.

I realise now that the saying about policemen looking younger can be extended to doctors.

The be spotted specimen in front of me had hardly started shaving and was dressed as though he had just popped in from a barbecue .

Well with this and other little niggles about appointment accessibility I decided to change surgeries.

This of course meant that I could have a medical MOT to see if I was fit for purpose.

I duly attended and had a blood sample taken(I did mention that I hadn't actual arrived to donate blood. Well it did seem a lot.)

There followed a blood pressure reading which was rather high. This in turn led to being fitted with blood a pressure monitor to be worn for a day. Every time this fired up, I lost the feeling in the fingers of my left hand.

I then re attended the surgery for the results, which again weren't good.

The doctor was a pleasant enough late twenties FY2 Doctor. Yes I wondered about that title.

He gently discussed the high readings and pointed out the possible likely serious health problems that could ensue if left untreated.

He also discussed the issuing of tablets to help control the problem along with a regime of diet and ,exercise and weight loss.

All well and good you may think? I would agree apart from the fact that he was sat there opposite me with all the appearance of a young Jabba the Hutt. Okay I slightly exaggerate.

To my untrained eye he looked like future A& E fodder, but as ever it was a case of do as I say not as I do.

I collected the prescription and started on the course of tablets.

I few days later (I am a man after all) I happened to read the instructions more thoroughly.

Three of the side effects listed were drowsiness, headaches and dizziness; which were the exact symptoms that I had related to the doctor on my consultation.

Is there some X -File type conspiracy going on here?

Time to get fit I think.

KEEPING FIT.

Having already attained the respectable age old codger's membership demands, your thoughts too may turn to keeping as fit as possible. There are several ways to do this.

You may join a gym, most will be full of young posers, but if selected wisely you can find a suitable niche.

You should of course cut your cloth accordingly building up to a sprightly shuffle.

The aim is for fitness and not membership of the stroke club. If you are lucky you will meet up with a like minded group who after an initial try at the keep fit lark(say around 15 minutes) will elect to decamp to the local hostelry.

Once you are there you can all reminisce about your long lost youth when it was threpence a pint and men were men and sheep were nervous!

Perhaps the cheapest method of keeping fit, is surely walking;
whether it be the afore mentioned shop browsing or the more
energetic street walking. No not that kind, you are well past your
potential attraction days.

You can spend hours wandering the streets smiling your amiable old
codger smile to each and every soul that you should meet.

It is perhaps wise to tone the smile down depending on the recipient;
young children and Police Officers can be spooked by a grimace that
they last saw with Heath Ledger's portrayal of 'The Joker' in the
'Dark Knight'.

No it's best to just nod slightly as you pass.

It is also inadvisable to do too many perimeter circuits of the local
High School. You risk either a meeting with the local law or more
likely become the target of some junior ne'er-do-well who is hanging
around his former school hoping to impress the 'chicks.'

So it is probably more advisable to head for the great outdoors. you
should dress accordingly for the vagaries of our great British climate.

But let's not overdo it!

THE END IS NIGH.

As you have retired you will, at the time of writing probably have achieved the age of 65 years(being a male codger and not a biddy). You have a couple of points to ponder; in this medically advanced age, government statistics state that you can expect another 21.6 years if you live in Kensington or Chelsea but this reduces to a figure of 15.9 years if you live in Manchester!

This flies in the face of the term 'Southern Softies' or is it that we work harder int' mill country?

There is a saying in these parts, 'hard work never killed anyone, but it made them some queer shapes!

This average increase in longevity is on the face of it welcome news, but I worry about the word average.

I know a splendid lady who has reached the age of 109 years old. This is both laudable and amazing but the worry is that she has lived past the conking out age for her generation by some 37 years. My question is has she pinched some of my years to attain this?

Bless her but fair's fair, give and take, swings and roundabouts etc. Can I sue?

I and my peers(first on the left down the steps sir) are lucky, those who are but a few years younger will work until they are 67-69 years old eventually.

Whilst the next generation will probably work until they drop, what next children in coal mines and stuffed up factory chimneys?

The increase in retirement age is particularly unfair and undesirable for women, they have my full support, after all someone needs to make my meals and do the housework.

Whilst on the topic of age related problems, have you tried to take out a Life Insurance policy at your advanced age?

I dipped my toe in this cesspit, I foolishly gave my mobile number to one Life Insurance provider, within a week I had some twenty calls from different companies mostly offering funeral plans.

My irritated response was, 'thank you, but no thank you!'

On further insistence from the bonus driven lackeys, my closing remark was to state that here in the U.K.I had never ever heard of anyone dying and being left unburied/cremated, had they?

The term 'old age' is misguiding ;though the joints creak and the eyesight fails, in my minds eye I still feel in my mid thirties. The feet still tap with an urge to dance to the music I grew up with. Tamala Motown, The Beatles, Elvis, Queen, Abba the list goes on, all evoke happy memories.

Having reached that peculiar time of life when the spirit and body is still willing to dance to these golden oldies. I find I can't.

I have passed through the embarrassing Dad Dancing stage progressed through to Uncle Flatfoot and eventually 'sit down Grandad' time of life.

Life can be cruel, but we must take our pleasure were we can.

As long as you have a roof over your head, good health and can pay the bills then my friend you have it made.

No more nine 'til five drudgery, you can do as you please(wife permitting),just get out there enjoy yourself!

Write a bucket list of things to do before you shuffle off the mortal coil; learn a new skill, go somewhere you have never been, do a sponsored skydive.

Well perhaps the last one is a bit O.T.T. but if you do, wear two layers of underwear. Think of the spectators!

Jeff Stevens.

Jeff Stevens.

Jeff Stevens.

Jeff Stevens.

Jeff Stevens.

ABOUT THE AUTHOR

As a newbie retiree I find after some 48 years of working to pay the bills, it's now the time to do something more enjoyable.
This booklet is a step in that direction.

15460452R00038

Printed in Great Britain
by Amazon